Original title:
The Meaning of Life According to Google

Copyright © 2025 Creative Arts Management OÜ
All rights reserved.

Author: Gideon Barrett
ISBN HARDBACK: 978-1-80566-199-3
ISBN PAPERBACK: 978-1-80566-494-9

Algorithms of Being

Life's a search engine, oh what a sight,
Queries for answers, day and night.
Forgot my password, what's my aim?
Google says focus, but I'm lost in the game.

Ping! A new thought, like a pop-up ad,
Stay on this page, don't be too mad.
Scrolling for wisdom, swipe left for fate,
Can I bookmark joy? Oh, isn't it great!

Digital Reflections on Purpose

Reflected in screens, I ponder my role,
What's the hashtag? Am I whole?
Pixels of purpose show on my feed,
But life's more than likes, or viral creed.

Searching for meaning in memes and tweets,
Each retweet a moment, each like a treat.
Is my soul a GIF, looping in space?
Or just another data point in cyberspace?

Keywords: Why Are We Here?

Typing my thoughts in a quest for the truth,
'Why are we here?' is the ultimate proof.
SEO says focus, earn some views,
But answers in slogans confuse the hues.

Bounce rate of meaning, that clicks in my brain,
Tagging my questions, but still feelin' plain.
Ads for enlightenment pop up so fast,
Can wisdom be purchased, or is that a bust?

Bytes of Enlightenment

In bytes we trust, let's crunch the data,
Happiness indexed? That can't be the beta.
Download a smile, it's a binary dream,
But life's more than pixels and flashy themes.

Processing joy with my coffee cup,
Uploading laughter, never give up.
Life's a download, an endless parade,
Where every bad pun is fundamentally made!

Virtual Puzzles of Life

In a world of clicks and swipes,
I search for answers in all types.
Google says, just ask away,
But I'm still lost, at least today.

I type my woes and hit 'enter',
The AI laughs, the screen a mentor.
It suggests I learn to cook, you see,
I guess that's wisdom—can't eat emoji!

Searching for Solace in Screens

I scroll through life with weary thumbs,
Hoping for wisdom from pixelated chums.
Each search leads to strange new quests,
    Like finding out why cats are best.

Advice from forums, memes galore,
Life's mysteries solved by a GIF or four.
In a sea of data, I float and weave,
    Who needs a guru when you got Steve?

The Digital Trail of Truth

In search of meaning, I went online,
Found wisdom wrapped in a punchline.
I learned life's deep, but also quite nutty,
Google, you've made my brain feel all fuzzy.

With every query, I dive deeper still,
From existential dread to recipes for thrill.
Each link a breadcrumb in this vast maze,
Leading me further in digital haze.

Undercurrents of the Internet

Beneath the surface, memes collide,
Each click a wave on the web's wild tide.
I ask for guidance, but what do I find?
A cat in a sweater, to chill my mind.

Life's a riddle, solved with a GIF,
No sage or prophet, just a viral lift.
In bytes of humor, we all can thrive,
Who knew that laughter helps us survive?

Reflections in a Glass Screen

Google gave me answers,
I asked my heart the same.
Digits danced in pixels,
Yet felt a tad mundane.

Searching for that secret,
I clicked on every link.
That life's a viral cat video,
Made me stop and think.

Queries and suggestions,
Pop-ups with every sigh.
A meme's profound wisdom,
Might just be the reason why.

In this digital jungle,
We stumble and we scroll.
Finding depth in hashtags,
While seeking for our soul.

Semantics of the Soul

I typed my woes in search bars,
Found wisdom wrapped in fun.
Life's just an algorithm,
Jokes pile up, one by one.

Keywords sharpen the focus,
On what I need to know.
Yet every time I ponder,
More questions seem to grow.

A quirk of auto-complete,
Chose the path less traveled.
Maybe truth's a riddle,
Not something to be unraveled.

When life hands me search terms,
I smile at Google's wit.
For every silly inquiry,
Isn't there a perfect fit?

Paths of Insight in Electric Spaces

In the web where we wander,
Questions fly like balloons.
Searching for deeper answers,
In email, memes, and tunes.

My spirit yearns for insights,
Yet I'm lost in the cloud.
Feeling smart with my searches,
But funny, a little loud.

Every click brings a choice,
But results can be absurd.
The truth feels like a quiz show,
Ridiculous and blurred.

So I'll laugh at my queries,
Finding joy in the game.
Life's a patchwork of nonsense,
That's how I learned its name.

Riddles of Existence in Silent Ones and Zeros

Deep in the code of being,
Existence softly hums.
On the search for meaning,
Life answers with a thumbs-up.

From pixels to profound thoughts,
I sift through bytes galore.
Yet Googling my intentions,
Left me wanting more.

It's funny how we ponder,
With every click we make.
In zeros and in ones,
Life's riddles shake and quake.

But with laughter in my heart,
I embrace the absurdity.
Searching for my purpose,
Is just digital curiosity.

Virtual Whispers of Wisdom

In the digital flow, wisdom does gleam,
A search bar awaits, like a quirky dream.
What is my purpose? Oh, let's find out,
With memes and cat photos, there's no room for doubt.

Click, click, click, the answers arise,
In articles spun from half-baked replies.
Life's just a quiz, no need to despair,
Just type in your woes; there's wisdom to share.

Navigating Existence Through Code

Life is a program, let's run and debug!
With algorithms acting as our trusty rug.
Error 404: purpose not found,
But playlists and TikToks keep spinning around.

Control, alt, delete—feelings erased,
In this cyber maze, we're all interlaced.
Endless updates, please reboot the grin,
Maybe existence is just a mad spin!

Riddles of Reality Online

Life's like a forum, where chaos has reign,
Scroll, scroll, scroll, but we can't feel the pain.
Ask a question, a thousand replies,
Yet wisdom gets lost in the digital skies.

What's the secret? Post something bizarre!
Memes might hold answers, scrolling afar.
In comment threads lie a jest or a clue,
Just don't take it seriously, that'd be taboo!

Tapping into the Cosmos

We're stardust and data, a cosmic blend,
Searching for meaning, is this all pretend?
Astronauts of laughter, we orbit in glee,
In spaces of pixels, we wander so free.

Staring at stars through our screens every night,
Who knew the universe lived just out of sight?
With hashtags for hope and emojis for cheer,
Can life be absurd? Oh dear, oh dear!

Wisdom Written in Keywords

In a world of clicks and taps,
We search for truths in digital maps.
Life's queries lead us in loops,
To memes and cat videos, to soothe the troops.

Ask for wisdom, follow the trends,
Reddit's sage advice never ends.
With every search, we lose our way,
But TikTok dances brighten the day.

Finding Nature in the Network

Trees and bees in pixelated dreams,
Scrolling through color-coded schemes.
Nature's wonders in 4K screens,
Filtered photos, all that gleams.

Wi-Fi signals in the breeze,
Notifications buzzing with ease.
But don't forget the outside view,
Where real-life nature says, "Hello to you!"

Endless Pages of Possibility

Google's got answers, or so they claim,
But what is life? Just a trending game.
Infinite links to spiral down,
Clicking 'next' in a digital town.

Yet sitting back and sipping tea,
Could be the best search for me.
For life's not just about the grind,
It's seeking laughter with peace of mind.

The Cosmic Search Engine

Stars aligned in a browser tab,
Searching for meaning, it's a little drab.
But gag reels show us what's profound,
Laughter echoes in cosmic sound.

A universe wide, yet so confined,
In quippy quotes, we seek to find.
Life's puzzle? It's all in jest,
With giggles leading us to rest.

Fractals of Fulfillment

In a world like a fractal, we twist and we turn,
Searching for answers, but what do we learn?
Cats on the internet, wisdom galore,
Life's greatest lesson—just meme and explore.

A click here, a scroll there, oh what a delight,
Life's messy equations, let's not get uptight.
Finding fulfillment in chaos and fun,
Like finding a pizza when you're on the run.

Threads of Reality Weaved

Threads intertwined in a tangled web,
Search for your purpose, but you're back to the ebb.
Reality's fabric is frayed and bizarre,
Just Google your questions; it'll take you far.

Life's a knit scarf made of random Yelp reviews,
Woven with wisdom and bytes of good news.
So laugh at the chaos, it's part of the art,
For each fraying thread is just a quirky part.

On the Dashboard of Destiny

On destiny's dashboard, we find many clicks,
Driving through life with hilarity's tricks.
Gaslight alarms and a map full of stars,
But all we want is to cruise in our cars.

Searching for shortcuts through the vast unknown,
Each time we detour, it leads us back home.
So buckle your seatbelt, let laughter abound,
For the joy of the journey is what we have found.

Navigating Life's Search History

Scrolling through memories, what have we sought?
Life's search history is hilariously fraught.
What's the best pizza? Or how to dance right?
Searching for meaning at two in the night.

Google knows wonders, but can't fetch the fun,
Like tripping on pillows when you're on the run.
So add to your queries, let curiosity flow,
For answers are fleeting, but laughter will grow.

Insights from the Digital Abyss

In queries we trust, with laughter at stake,
What's five plus two? A funny mistake!
Life's secrets unveiled, just a click and a sigh,
Turns out it's pizza, that's the reason why!

Searching for wisdom, we scroll ever fast,
But memes fill the gaps, in a world that's a blast.
'What's the best way to live?' we type in a rush,
And Google responds, 'In pajamas, don't hush!'

Holograms of Happiness

They say life's a joke, we're all just a bit,
With search bars aglow and a humorous wit.
Type in 'how to smile', you'll see it appear,
A hologram of laughter, the best one, I fear!

With pixels that dance, we find joy in a meme,
Like finding a donut in a virtual dream.
So ask for a reason, and what will you find?
Just a GIF of a cat, oh how life is kind!

The Universal Query Unveiled

What is the point? We ask night and day,
Google just chuckles and says, 'Eat hay!'
A search for enlightenment brings up a quiz,
And asks for your favorite cheese, how bizarre is this?

Life's an equation, but math makes me yawn,
It's simpler with tacos at the break of dawn.
In the end, it seems, if we really must know,
The answer is laughter, and on that we can grow!

Data-Driven Dreams

In the realm of data, our dreams intertwine,
Searching for goldfish in bottles of wine.
"What should I do?" we type with a grin,
And find it suggests, 'Just let the fun begin!'

With charts and with graphs, we follow the trend,
Even if it leads to a cat meme, my friend.
So let's raise a glass to our virtual guide,
And embrace the chaos, let humor abide!

The Search for Significance

In a cloud of keywords, we dive,
Searching for meaning to feel alive.
Are we just data, or something more?
Clicking for joy on every byte's shore.

Life's a query, a search so grand,
With every answer, we misunderstand.
Did that cat meme teach me to be kind?
Or just waste my time with a glitchy bind?

Pixels of wisdom, or just a joke,
Between the lines, we laugh and poke.
Do we exist on a digital plane?
Or just echo screams of our own mundane?

With each new click, we ponder still,
Does our true worth depend on skill?
In this vast network, we find our cheer,
Life's just a meme that we all adhere.

Reflections in the Cloud

Up in the ether, what do we see?
A cloud of questions, a digital spree.
Searching for answers with nothing to lose,
Typing in hopes, but we get confused.

Do we exist in binary code?
Or are we just data on a heavy load?
Clicking each link, a hamster on wheels,
Life's just a search that no one reveals.

In the great web of life, we scroll,
Finding our way through the data hole.
Is wisdom found in aggregating likes?
Or in the silly dance of baby bikes?

Oh, endless queries, with laughter abound,
In this vast ocean, we often drown.
From memes that enlighten to gifs that thrill,
Life's a big joke, a viral drill.

Ethereal Answers in Binary

On digital waves, we make our plea,
Oh wise Google, won't you answer me?
Is my purpose lost in the endless stream?
Or just a punchline in a meme-filled dream?

With every search, I giggle and click,
What's my true calling? Is it this trick?
Each result a riddle wrapped in a pun,
The wisdom I'm after seems so far from fun.

In code we trust, our hopes take flight,
Is enlightenment merely a search at night?
Are chips and bytes the keys to grace?
Or is it just pizza and an online race?

With pixels as my compass, I roam,
In cyberspace, I search for home.
And if existence is just a byte,
Give me the punchline, make it light!

The Wisdom of Crowds

In forums and threads, we gather round,
The wisdom of crowds in giggles is found.
Ask any question, watch them respond,
In this online jungle, we all bond.

"Why are we here?" I post with glee,
And wait for the masses to find it for me.
But answers vary from profound to bizarre,
As I scroll through wisdom from near and far.

With every reply, I chuckle and sigh,
From depth of meaning to "Just eat pie."
Life's great purpose, a quest so absurd,
In the chaos of comments, my voice is unheard.

Yet among the memes and confusing advice,
I find my joy in this digital slice.
For laughter connects us, so one may suppose,
In this wild web, true meaning grows.

A Journey Through Infinite Links

Click, scroll, and type away,
Life's a search, what do they say?
From cat memes to deep advice,
All wisdom's wrapped in a link device.

Google's wise and sometimes quirky,
Answers found, but often murky.
Left wondering with every click,
Is it truth or just a trick?

With every search, a new tale spins,
In this game, where do we begin?
A dozen tabs, still in the fray,
Where's the meaning? Who can say?

Yet we laugh, and find delight,
In every query, every bite.
Life's a joke, or so it seems,
In every search for bigger dreams.

Serendipity in Search Results

Type away, what will I find?
Perhaps an answer, or just a grind.
A recipe for a cake I've missed,
Or tips on how to coexist.

Unexpected joy in every search,
A squirrel's dance, or an old church.
Stumbling 'cross things that make you grin,
Like how to train your pet, or win.

Life's a riddle wrapped in code,
Like a pop-up ad that's really bold.
Why not laugh, and take a peek,
At the chaos we all seek?

With every click, a flip of fate,
A new adventure to navigate.
What will we find, what will we do?
Just hit "search," and start anew!

Pixels of Purpose

In the web of life, we wade,
Pixels bounce like a playful braid.
What's my purpose? Time to check,
Clicking links, feeling the wreck.

Found a meme that speaks my soul,
Turns out 'existence' is just a scroll.
Through belly laughs and quirky chats,
I ponder life with all my spats.

Rows of search results fill my screen,
What's real, what's just a dream?
Is it profound or just for fun?
In every click, I'm on the run!

Life's a pixelated mess, you see,
Yet here I am, just trying to be.
So, raise a glass to every link,
That helps us laugh more than we think!

Defining Existence in Hyperlinks

Hyperlink here, hyperlink there,
Defining life like we're a pair.
From how-to guides to motivational talks,
Life's a quest with endless walks.

How to find myself, here's a hint,
Just search for humor in the print.
Life's an answer that's yet to load,
With pop-ups that lighten the road.

Got lost in a maze of meme-filled delight,
Where we laugh and dance through the night.
Existence found in laugh tracks and sighs,
Navigating life through witty replies.

So here's to the links that set us free,
In every error, there's comedy.
Find your path through the pixel haze,
And bask in the laughter of life's wild ways!

Searching for Solace

In a search bar overflowing with dreams,
I typed my woes, it seems.
A million answers, all so vague,
Is life's true meaning in a snazzy plague?

I asked if I'm a star in the sky,
But Google said, "Just drink chai."
A cat meme popped up, oh great,
Now is that wisdom or just bait?

Philosophers buzz like flies,
In my inbox, where reason dies.
So I click 'I'm Feeling Lucky', in vain,
To find the gems amongst the grain.

I close the tab, my quest in tow,
For solace found in the Web's show.
Through gifs and laughter, I start to see,
Life's true joy is just to be free.

Truths Hidden in the SERP

I typed in 'What's the point of this?',
Google replied with a puppy kiss.
Between ads for shoes and fishy sights,
I found a riddle wrapped in bytes.

Half the time it offered a meme,
About life's essence in an ice cream.
"Just enjoy it," the pixels screamed,\nWhile I wondered if I'd even dreamed.

With keywords lost in endless scroll,
What's life's purpose? A Google troll?
"Just keep searching," my browser sang,
As I pondered if my head would hang.

A dozen tabs open in a whirl,
In the chaos, my thoughts unfurl.
Maybe life's just a curious test,
With Google here, I'll jest my best.

Navigating the Web of Wonder

I sailed the seas of cyberspace,
Sought wisdom in a dog's face.
With every click, confusion grew,
Life's great quest reduced to 'who knew?'

"What is joy?" I asked the page,
It laughed and linked a cat meme stage.
While wisdom hunts in a pixel parade,
Searching leads to cookies displayed.

One answer pointed towards a fish,
"Live your life, and always swish."
With every riddle, new tabs zing,
As Google plays philosopher king.

Through pop-ups and those cool sound bites,
The meaning's lost in synthetic lights.
So I smile, as I navigate this spin,
Life's a game, let the laughter begin.

Answers in the Matrix of Meaning

In the digital realm, I find my quest,
A matrix of queries vying for the best.
"What's my purpose?" I seek from the core,
But Google chuckles, "Just eat more lore!"

I clicked on 'life hacks' to locate clues,
But ended up with tips on color blues.
"Dance like nobody's watching," it preached,\nWhile my other browser windows screeched.

From health tips to lost sock advice,
Every answer comes with a sprinkle of spice.
"Thou shalt binge-watch," the wisdom blares,
In the end, it's all just computer flares.

So amidst the noise and digital fright,
I chuckle and grin at the meme-filled sight.
Life's a riddle wrapped in a URL,
And together, we're navigating quite well.

The Search for Significance

In every click, a question lies,
Is there a scheme behind our sighs?
With memes and gifs, we roam the net,
Searching for truths we can't forget.

The algorithms spin with grace,
Yet wisdom hides in cyberspace.
A cat video or life advice,
Which one will add to our paradise?

We type 'What's life?' and hit return,
A million hits, yet none discern.
So we'll laugh and scroll all night,
Chasing answers, what a sight!

In digital realm, we find our thrill,
The search is fun, it gives a chill.
Are we lost or on our way?
Google knows, or so they say!

Perception in the Age of Information.

With screens aglow, our vision's blurred,
We ponder life, a bit absurd.
Clicking links with hopeful dreams,
Are we more than data streams?

We browse for wisdom, sound and sage,
Yet TikTok dances steal the stage.
In viral trends, we seek the truth,
But end up lost in TikTok youth.

What gives us joy? What brings us peace?
In bytes and pixels, minds release.
Are answers found in clever memes?
Or left behind in shattered dreams?

So swipe and scroll, and don't dismay,
Perception's weird in this wild play.
With every click, a laugh, a frown,
In endless loops, we spin around!

Search Engines and Soul Journeys

We type in queries, bold and bright,
Hoping to find some guiding light.
'How to live?' the search declares,
Tangled in a web of digital lairs.

Results come up in heaps and piles,
Guidance served with goofy smiles.
Yoga tips or cooking hacks?
What's more profound? Who even tracks?

We seek our paths in endless scroll,
Each keyword fed into our soul.
A recipe or a sage's quote,
Are we lost or just remote?

With every search, our minds expand,
Yet wisdom's buried in quicksand.
We laugh and learn in cyberspace,
For every journey's just a race!

Queries of Existence Unraveled

Questions fly like digital birds,
'What is meaning?' and other words.
With every tap, we chase the clue,
Are answers real, or just a view?

In a world of spam and chatty bots,
We ponder life in every slot.
'Why am I here?'—the search begins,
Yet it's lost between the spins.

A funny TikTok steals the show,
While deep thoughts hide behind the glow.
We swirl in laughter, hope, and doubt,
And wonder what it's all about.

But in the chaos, joy is found,
In every meme, our hearts rebound.
So query on, with zest and glee,
For life's a ride, on a digital spree!

The Infinite Scroll of Thought

I searched for answers late at night,
But all I found were memes in sight.
Wisdom lost in digital haze,
Endless scroll, a pixel maze.

I clicked through life, no map to see,
Life hacks told me, 'Just be free!'
Fortune cookies on my screen,
Told me laughter's what I mean.

In this quest, I found a cat,
Who knew far more than my old brat.
It sat and stared, with wisdom bold,
'Just chase the red dot,' it told.

So here I am, with giggles bright,
Life's little quirks, a silly flight.
For deep in searches, what I've learned,
Is joy in clicks, and fun I've earned.

In the Archive of Humanity

Diving deep in data seas,
I stumbled on some ancient bees.
Their dances showed, in circles spun,
Life's just sweet—now go have fun!

In archives vast, I found some sage,
Whose wisdom filled a single page.
He whispered low, through wires long,
'Of life's great truths, just sing your song.'

I typed, I poked, and I clicked around,
Answers buzzing without a sound.
Yet all I found, 'twixt links and streams,
Was laughter echoing in my dreams.

So here's the gist, the cosmic scoop,
Life's not a task, it's one big loop.
Jump in the fun, embrace the chase,
In every scroll, find joy's embrace.

Clicks and Contemplations

In the web of thoughts, I lost my way,
With every click, I felt the sway.
Philosophers in pixels yell,
Telling me life's a grand carousel.

I pondered hard, yet found I'd see,
A talking dog from Tennessee.
He wagged his tail and said with glee,
'Fetch your dreams and set them free!'

Through endless pages, I did roam,
A Google search was not a home.
But every giggle, every jest,
Taught me that life's a funny quest.

So I'll embrace each silly line,
In this wild ride, I feel divine.
A digital dance in bytes so bright,
Life searches on, a pure delight.

Data Streams of Desire

Caught in streams of endless data,
I sought for wisdom, but found a beta.
Algorithms twist and turn in jest,
Yet in their chaos, I found my rest.

A query posed on how to thrive,
Returned a book on how to jive.
So now I dance in bits and bytes,
Living life like wild delights.

The graphs went up, then down, oh dear,
I followed trends, but found no fear.
For in the crunch of numbers bright,
I laughed and twirled through day and night.

So here I am, a happy glitch,
Just clicking on what brings the itch.
Life's a stream, a data chase,
Let's surf the waves, and find our place.

Algorithms as Artisans

In code they weave, the builders of dreams,
Crafting life's questions, or so it seems.
With clicks we ask, and they reply,
But sometimes wonder, why oh why?

From cat pics to wisdom, a never-ending scroll,
Searching for answers, we're trying to roll.
Yet lost in the data, we laugh and we cry,
Is life just a meme? Let's give it a try!

They calculate love, as if it's a game,
With numbers and letters, we're all just the same.
In this binary circus, we dance in delight,
Life's just algorithms, oh what a sight!

So raise up your glasses, for search engines bright,
Crafting our journeys, bringing us light.
In this quirky world of clicks and bold flair,
Let's toast to our lives, found everywhere!

A Click Away from Clarity

In a sea of results, clarity ships,
With humor and quirk, we navigate trips.
Type in your woes, hit return in a rush,
Waiting for wisdom, in a digital hush.

A chirpy reply pops up quick as a flash,
Telling us truths, or just making a splash.
'Life's just a puzzle,' the search bar does say,
But can it fix socks? Or guide our way?

As we scroll through the wisdom of countless minds,
We giggle at answers that cleverly binds.
Yet in the chaos, we find some sweet glee,
The search for life's purpose is a search for some tea!

So here's to the clicks, the laughs and the tries,
For every wild answer brings brightening sighs.
In this giggle-filled voyage through data we roam,
We find out our questions are leading us home!

Texts of Transcendence

Scroll back to the start, what was it we sought?
A nugget of joy, or an easy jackpot?
The texts all confound, yet tickle our brains,
In the awkwardness, wisdom quietly reigns.

With hashtags of hope and emojis of cheer,
We parse through the phrases, confusion draws near.
Life is a hashtag, a trend, or a joke,
In this digital realm, even profundities poke.

The queries we type, all laced with some spice,
Like, 'What's the key to a longer life's slice?'
But the keyboard just chuckles, in witty despair,
While we keep on typing with love and with care.

So let's share a laugh, in this code-riddled quest,
As we dig through the texts that make us feel blessed.
For each tiny answer might lighten the strife,
In the grand tapestry that we call our life!

Existence Encoded in Search Bars

What is this life? Let's check and confirm,
In pixels and bytes, we watch wisdom squirm.
We type in our troubles, hit enter with glee,
As algorithms chuckle, they're deeper than we.

Our existential musings, reduced to a link,
A click that might make you rethink your drink.
With each search we take, it's a whimsical dive,
To decipher existence, we must first revive.

From 'Why am I here?' to 'How many carbs?'
Search engines echo our most curious garbs.
They serve us up answers, more questions arise,
As we scroll and we ponder, with wonder in our eyes.

So here's to the queries, the jests that we share,
In the vast world of search, with humor laid bare.
As we chase all the answers, let's remember to smile,
For existence is quirky, and so is our style!

Intersections of Ideas

In a world of memes and gifs,
We find wisdom in the rifts.
Ask the questions, seek the fun,
Searching answers, never done.

Late-night thoughts and silly pics,
Philosophers with clever tricks.
Every click a brand new thought,
Life's a puzzle, tightly caught.

From cat videos to deep debates,
Who knew wisdom has such traits?
In our search for sense and peace,
We laugh, connect, and find release.

URL to the Universe

Scrolling through the endless links,
Finding answers, who dares blink?
Life's a search bar, sleek and neat,
With every click, it's bittersweet.

Queries wide, from love to fate,
Each new page sounds like a date.
In the cyberspace we drift and roam,
A modern heart, yet far from home.

Every blog a cosmic tease,
Finding meaning with such ease.
Just hit refresh, don't miss a beat,
The universe is at our feet.

Clickbait Connections

Seven ways to find your spark,
Nine reasons life's a quirky lark.
Oh look! A list that seems so true,
A viral post, we're into you.

Watch now: a secret's been revealed,
A hidden truth, almost concealed.
Life's a game of what to click,
Finding joy in every trick.

With headlines bold and graphs so bright,
We dance along the digital light.
Though questions sway, the answers jig,
In this circus, we all dig.

Current of Consciousness Online

What's the meaning? What's the deal?
Scrolling memes that make us squeal.
Philosophy in every post,
We laugh, we wonder, raise a toast!

Say cheese! The universe is wide,
In hashtags, we take our ride.
Every tweet a joke or grand,
With wisdom shared across the land.

Digital thoughts, a vast swell,
Life's a story, hard to tell.
But in laughter, we find our way,
Connecting hearts in bright array.

Search Queries of Existence

Why am I here? I can't find,
A single answer, just memes combined.
Clicking through pages, what a delight,
Life's just a txt, not black and white.

Cats on my screen, wisdom they share,
A sage in a box, with fur and a stare.
Searching for meaning, a quest so grand,
The fridge is empty, I just need a hand.

Internet trolls and clever bots,
They ponder existence while searching for spots.
Query by query, I scroll through and sigh,
Maybe it's all just a clever lie.

So thumbs up for each click that I make,
With hopes that some enlightenments shake.
In this vast net, where info runs rife,
I'll laugh with the pixels, that's my real life.

Bytes of Being

In the realm of bytes, I seek to find,
What makes this chaos feel so aligned.
Is it friendship, or just a good meme?
Life's like a code, or so it would seem.

Pixels and passions collide in my brain,
As I search for meaning like a runaway train.
A cookie or two, for wisdom they plead,
But all I get are ads for dog food and seed.

Feeling existential, I type with glee,
Searching for answers, can it really be?
Connection or isolation, it's hard to tell,
In cyberspace, we're all under this spell.

Life's just a network, click here and there,
No Wi-Fi, no meaning? Oh, what a despair!
Yet with each new search, I chuckle and grin,
In this amusing quest, I keep logging in.

Algorithmic Reflections

With algorithms buzzing, life's a grand show,
Finding our purpose, like where did it go?
Typed in my doubts, pressed enter with flair,
Hoping the search bar will finally care.

Caught in a loop of profound queries,
"What's it all mean?" my screen softly tearies.
Results pop up, a blend of pure gold,
But mostly just cat pics, stories retold.

Chasing reflections in a digital sea,
Finding my purpose in an emoji spree.
Life's an equation of laughs and of tears,
A glitch here and there can lead to new cheers.

So as I scroll through life's playful charade,
I'll dance with the pixels, my worries will fade.
In this machine, so bright and so wild,
I'll revel in humor, like a curious child.

Digital Echoes of Purpose

In the echo of pixels, my purpose does ring,
Searching for truth in this digital bling.
With each little beep, and each light that glows,
I wonder aloud as the Wi-Fi flows.

Gigabytes of laughter, I glean from the net,
Usernames and memes I won't soon forget.
Mankind's quest wrapped in a funny quirk,
Life's a bad hashtag, oh what a perk!

Life's just a post, with likes and retweets,
A stream of connections, where chaos competes.
What is my purpose? Oh, let's just assume,
I'll scroll and I'll laugh in this pixelated room.

So here's to the searches, and all that they yield,
The quirks of our lives that the web has revealed.
In digital echoes, we stumble and play,
Laughing through life in this quirky ballet.

Insights from the Web

In the search bar, I typed my plight,
Is it cake, or am I light?
Life's a puzzle, click and scroll,
Finding answers takes a toll.

Google says, just live and laugh,
Count your memes, not your gaffs,
Cats and dogs bring joy, they claim,
I'm just here to play their game.

Query for wisdom, oh what a thrill,
But the best advice comes from a grill,
A recipe for peace, how profound,
Life's a feast, and love's the sound.

So here's to searches, wild and bright,
Each click reveals a new delight,
In the vast web we play, we see,
Life's just fun, so let it be!

Echoes of Inquiry

Questions echo like a dance,
Type and click, give life a chance,
What's my purpose? What's the score?
Is it just pizza and some more?

Online answers rare and strange,
Life's a riddle, never plain,
Scroll through memes, find some cheer,
Deep thoughts come after a beer.

Videos of dogs saving the day,
Teach me more than philosophers say,
Like wise owls in a techy age,
I'm just turning a knowledge page.

So let's embrace the silly quest,
As we search and laugh, we're blessed,
Life's a giggle, bright and loud,
Finding wisdom in the crowd!

Digging Deep in a Sea of Information

Down the rabbit hole I dive,
A mountain of data keeps me alive,
With memes and facts swirling around,
Searching for meaning that's often drowned.

In a sea of links, I find delight,
Yoga, cat videos, all seem right,
Philosophy's mixed with a sprinkle of fun,
Life's a party, we've just begun.

But seriously, what's the big deal?
Is it wisdom or just a meal?
Wrap it up in digital threads,
And share laughs before we hit our beds.

So as I dig through bytes and trends,
I find connection, where laughter bends,
Life's just pixels that spark and flow,
Let's embrace this curious show!

Searching for Connection

With a swipe and a tap, I search for friends,
In the vast web where the laughter bends,
Life's a chatroom, come and engage,
Finding joy outside a cage.

Keywords and phrases, they twist and turn,
In the quest for connection, I yearn,
But all I find are dancing cats,
And a million jokes about silly hats.

From deep thoughts to memes that slay,
Life's one big party, in disarray,
Connections woven with links and shares,
Let's log in to see what cares.

So here's to the search, oh what a ride,
In laughter and fun, let's take pride,
Life's a mystery, full of fun,
Together in chaos, we will run!

Local Buffers of the Mind

In a world of thought and space,
Information races, a dizzying chase.
Questions pop up, like ads on a screen,
Searching for wisdom, but what does it mean?

Click, scroll, and swipe through the maze,
Each answer unfolds in a myriad of ways.
Yet why do we ponder, what's lurking behind,
The buffers of life, they're not quite aligned!

We ask for some guidance, a tip from the fate,
But all that we find is 'Check back, it's late!'
The search engine chuckles, with algorithms so spry,
Hiding the secrets that float in the sky.

So here we are, in a digital whirl,
Seeking the truth, but life gives a twirl.
With data and memes to make us all grin,
The local buffers just want to fit in!

The Social Network of Sentience

Once more, I logged in to read all the thoughts,
Updates from friends, life's haphazard knots.
Caught in this web of alluring delight,
The sentience dances, both day and night.

Posts filled with selfies, and cats on a spree,
What matters most? Is it you or me?
Likes and shares fly through the air,
But what's the real reason we're all standing here?

Zooming through feeds, our thumbs a-twitch,
Chasing the likes, are we all just a glitch?
Scroll and reenact, our lives on display,
Yet laughing with friends is still here to stay.

In pixels and memes, deep connections we find,
But the social network can break, oh so blind.
For in the end, what makes life so bright,
Are the hugs, not the likes that gleam in the light!

Syntax of Selfhood

Life's a script, with lines we recite,
Syntax and grammar dance in the night.
What am I saying? Is it 'me' or 'we'?
In the text of existence, what can we see?

Verbs of ambition, nouns of despair,
Punctuation pauses, giving us air.
Adjectives sparkle, like stars in the dark,
But sometimes they fizzle—just snuff out the spark.

I write my own manual, edit with flair,
Mix metaphors wildly, as if I don't care.
In the story I pen, there's a plot twist or two,
With laughter and chaos, and a hiccup or who?

So, let's rhyme together if you feel the same,
In this syntax of self, there's joy—not just blame.
Scripted or spontaneous, we'll find our own role,
The play of existence, now that's the goal!

Rants, Rambles, and Renderings

Grab a coffee, let's chatter away,
Rants about life, come on, don't delay!
From traffic to tacos, we'll cover it all,
With rambles of nonsense, let's have a ball!

Oh, the renderings of life, they can baffle and stain,
Like socks in the wash, all mixed up in the rain.
We search for connection, for meaning, for laughs,
Yet often we stumble on unworthy paths.

Share all your gripes, let's laugh till we cry,
The drama of living is worth a good try.
For inside our rants, there's truth wrapped with glee,
In this fiesta of life, just let it all be!

So raise up your cup to the wild and absurd,
In rants, rambles, renderings—just let it be heard.
Life's funny and wacky, a slippery ride,
With laughter the compass, let joy be our guide!

Metaphors in Metadata

In pixels we ponder, in bytes we confide,
Life's riddles wrapped in a digital tide.
To click is to seek, to scroll is to roam,
Searching for wisdom, we sit by our chrome.

Oh, what is our purpose, the query displays?
'Take it easy!' it says, in a digital haze.
But with cat memes and tips on how to bake,
Is life but a joke or a grand cosmic prank?

In hashtags we gather, our truths do collide,
As we post our deep thoughts on the Cybernetic ride.
Like Wi-Fi connections, sometimes strong, sometimes weak,
We sift through the noise, just to feel unique.

So next time you search for profound insight,
Remember the fun in the data delight.
With laughter and clicks, navigate with glee,
Life's just a meme, or maybe it's free!

Questions in the Cloud

Questions like birds, in the cloud they take flight,
From 'Why am I here?' to 'Is Pluto still right?'
With a tap and a swipe, we find the profound,
But end up with answers that are silly, not sound.

From whether to diet to life hacks on scene,
To searching for meaning in a pumpkin spice dream.
Each query a puzzle, a riddle so bright,
Yet always distracted by the next viral bite.

Who knew that existence might hinge on a meme?
Or that all of this searching might just be a scheme?
With wisdom of crowds, or maybe just noise,
Life's like a phone—full of apps, not just toys.

So laugh at the questions that float in the sky,
We're all just data in the great cosmic fry.
In a cloud of confusion, we're searching for cheer,
But jokes are the answers—let's give them a cheer!

The Digital Compass of Self

Navigating life with a digital map,
But all that I find leads to more of a trap.
What's the best route? A GPS guide,
Yet every new path feels like an ego ride.

To post or to ponder, which calls me today?
A selfie at brunch, then I'm lost on the way.
Is my soul in my tweets, or tucked in my feels?
The compass spins wildly as it clicks on my reels.

With each swipe I seek, a new version appears,
A pixelated profile that counters my fears.
But does Wi-Fi connect me to who I should be,
Or is just another fork in my binary tree?

So here's to the journey, the searches we make,
Through hashtags of wisdom, through memes that awake.

Life as a gigabyte, so wild and absurd,
In the digital desert, we're still undeterred!

Trawling for Truth

In the net of the web, I fish for a sign,
With bait made of queries, and hopes that align.
Each link that I click, a new tale unfolds,
But truth feels elusive, just like shimmering gold.

'What is life's meaning?' I type with a grin,
And await the wisdom that I hope lies within.
A cat does a backflip, a dog wears a hat,
Yet I'm still left wondering, where's the life spat?

In the depths of the globe, with each passing wave,
I delve into chaos, it's truth that I crave.
Yet the fish that I catch are all tiny and stale,
A reminder that wisdom is lost in the trail.

So here's to the laughter, the bafflement bright,
In the ocean of info, we navigate light.
For in searching for meaning, we trip and we fall,
And sometimes that laughter could just be it all!

Server Farms and Soulmates

In circuits and cables, love's a dance,
A search for affection, a pixel romance.
Friend request hearts, we swipe and we scroll,
Does Wi-Fi connect us, or just take a toll?

In data we trust, yet crave human touch,
A robust connection, but not too much.
Love in a server, can it be true?
Or just bits and bytes in a virtual zoo?

Now Tinder is tangled in bits of my heart,
Matching with laughter, a digital start.
From memes to dreams, it's all quite a ride,
In the heart of the web is where I confide.

So here's to the coders who know all the codes,
In this quirky world where the humor explodes.
Let's laugh as we wander through bandwidth and clay,
Finding giggles in every place that we play.

Bits of Being

In bytes we find purpose, or so it is said,
Scrolling through life with our eyes slightly red.
From posts about brunch to cat videos near,
This digital journey just tickles the rear.

In hashtags we trust, for wisdom divine,
'Live, laugh, love' or 'Let's all sip some wine.'
Bytes of existence in memes do abound,
Encouraging laughs with each scroll up and down.

Searching for answers in Google's embrace,
But why is there traffic? Where's the fun place?
For every deep question, there's a joke to find,
Just hit search and chuckle, it'll open your mind.

Life's just a program, so glitchy and bright,
But hey, follow the humor, and everything's right.
From viral sensations to comments that sting,
In this byte-sized existence, we laugh and we sing.

Webbed Wonderings

In the network of life, we ponder and prod,
Questioning purpose, is it all just a facade?
Click-bait reflections, we dive and we thread,
Finding the punchline where logic has fled.

Lost in the web, we roam without map,
While life sends us memes that make us all clap.
From trailers of movies to tips on a cat,
Existence is goofy, much like where we sat.

With browsers and search bars guiding our quest,
We're seeking the wisdom in gifs, at best.
Yet through circuits and screens, we still yearn to see,
If there's more out there than this meme jubilee.

So let's raise a toast to these bytes we adore,
In wisdom and laughter, let our spirits soar.
With questions that wander and playful replies,
Perhaps the true answer is laughter, not sighs.

The Path Beyond Pixels

Walking through life, with a screen for a guide,
Finding a purpose, or at least some pride.
In forums we ask, and the answers flow wide,
Yet still feel alone, like a cloud on a ride.

Life's like a video game, full of quests,
Unlocking those moments, we're never at rest.
With jokes as our health bar, we stumble and fall,
But power-ups come from good memes after all.

Searching for meaning in algorithms deep,
Yet laughter is currency that we gladly keep.
From all of our blunders, we learn as we go,
Turning every dead end to a stand-up show.

So here's to the journey, both whimsical and wild,
With humor our compass, let's never be filed.
For in this grand pixelated universe roam,
We find all the answers; together, we're home.

Navigating the Essence

In the search bar I typed with glee,
'What's the point of you and me?'
Google chuckled, then spat some links,
'Enjoy the ride, just don't overthink!'

From memes to cats, it's all a must,
Life's just clicks, in search we trust!
With every scroll, I feel more spry,
Like I can fly, if only I try!

But then my laptop started to lag,
'Is this my life?' I started to brag.
Jumped on Reddit, made a new post,
Turns out it's just about what you coast!

So here I sit, with crumbs on my shirt,
Life's just a game, trying to convert.
A world of pixels, a floating hype,
Navigate easy, just swipe right, type!

Wisdom in the User's Query

A question asked, a quick response,
'Why are we here?' through pixel-dense bonds.
Google laughed, replied with a pun,
'You're just a blip in a digital run!'

Look deeper now? No, let's just stare,
At memes and clips, who really cares?
If life's a riddle wrapped in a jest,
Just take a selfie, let your smile fest!

Search for love, or that perfect shoe,
'What is joy?' lets click on view!
A parade of answers, a pixelated dance,
Scroll through life, and take a chance!

So here's the scoop, and I'm not shy,
Google's wisdom—just eat some pie.
Happiness isn't about grand schemes,
But simply enjoying your wildest dreams!

A Journey through Hyperlinks

Click here, then there, what's next on my map?
Life's but a journey, with a digital gap.
From one link to another, I skip like a stone,
Chasing answers in a world of unknown!

Loading times sometimes make me frown,
Is that a life lesson? Let's break it down.
Patience is key, or so they say,
But I'd rather have cookies, right here, right away!

Page after page, my quest seems bizarre,
Searching for wisdom, I scroll near and far.
An ad for shoes? I'll take that too,
Who knew self-discovery could come with a view?

Viral dances and epic fails,
Life's just a playlist, with curious trails.
So take the leap, don't fear the click,
Just remember, it's all just a quirky trick!

The Reality Check Box

Checked my answers, what's the catch?
Life's a riddle you can't quite match.
Google said, 'It's complicated, dear,'
I just want pizza and a cup of cheer!

Typed in my woes, hit enter then sigh,
Life hacks abound, as pixels fly by.
'How to be happy?' Oh, let's explore,
But first, can we focus on snacks galore?

The box of reality says life's a spree,
Not all answers come free as a decree.
Sometimes a cat meme just does the trick,
Scroll, laugh, repeat—oh, life's a quick flick!

So here's the truth, my browser reveals,
It's all about laughing, and sharing good meals.
With a wink and a grin, let the questions flow,
Life's just a search—let's go with the flow!

The Map of Mortality

Life is a quest, a grand old spree,
With questions like, 'What's the best recipe?'
We search for maps, but all that we find,
Is directions to places we've left far behind.

A goof with a graph, a pie chart that spins,
Google suggests, 'Just search for some wins!'
In the quest for more, we often lose sight,
Of sofa time, snacks, and the well-deserved night.

We ask, 'What's it all for?' while scrolling away,
But cat memes and movies sure brighten our day.
With clicks and with taps, we ponder the score,
Yet life's just a dance on an unending floor.

So embrace the absurd, let the laughter ignite,
In the chaos of searching, hold humor tight.
For any grand answer, we just might discover,
Is hidden in giggles, and that's worth the bother.

Pings of Purpose

We ping off our doubts, anxiously say,
'Is love in the air? Or just Wi-Fi decay?'
Life buzzes along like a phone on the fritz,
With notifications clamoring, causing some fits.

We seek out some wisdom in form of a tweet,
But all that we find are some memes that repeat.
With wisdom's a hashtag, we scroll through the feed,
And wonder if life's just a catalog of need.

In moments of calm, alerts start to chime,
'Find yourself!' they say, 'Life's a wait for the dime!'
Yet sought after purpose may come with a laugh,
In the search for it all, who forgot the giraffe?

So let's giggle and poke through the data we find,
That purpose has pings, and they're one of a kind.
Perhaps in each blooper, each moment of grace,
We find that the meaning can't be stitched in place.

Fragments of Fulfillment

Life's like a puzzle, we piece it each day,
With fragments of joy that float anyway.
We Google our feelings, 'What brings me delight?'
And find it's just pizza at the end of the night.

Each fragment we gather, a quirky affair,
A laugh with a buddy, a cat that can stare.
We chase after echoes, and search for the gold,
Yet cherish the stories that never grow old.

In snippets of laughter, our hearts intertwine,
With memes that uplift and a good glass of wine.
When fulfillment seems fractured, we simply cannot see,
That it's all in the moments, not just in the spree.

So piece it together, let happiness reign,
In the bits of our lives, joy's there to sustain.
For in every small heartbeat, a treasure does lie,
A mix of the mundane that helps us to fly.

Eclipsed by Search Results

In a world full of clicks and a whirlwind of tabs,
We seek out the answers, but end up with drabs.
What's the meaning they ask, with a search bar so bright,
Yet we laugh through the listings, in silly delight.

We type out our woes, with a hopeful intent,
But algorithms mock with each phrase that we sent.
Yet hidden in colors, amidst videos and GIFs,
We discover the fun embedded in rifts.

Perhaps life's not trapped in a daunting long quest,
But in silly distractions that help us the best.
We grin at the chaos of midnight run rants,
Finding joy in the mess, in our quirky old pants.

So let's cling to the laughter, the quirks, and the fun,
Let's dance through the questions, let's bask in the sun.
For the answers we seek, as we aim for the flow,
Are wrapped in the laughter we share as we go.

The Clicked Path to Understanding

I searched for wisdom, oh where to start?
The answers came quick, but none hit the heart.
'Life is a meme,' the screen brightly claimed,
Click this link for joy, or that's what it aimed.

I scrolled through questions, too many to read,
'Why are we here?' a curious seed.
'Is it true that cats are the rulers of fate?'
A search for the truth left me rather irate.

In endless tabs, confusion did grow,
Each click a new puzzle, making me slow.
But laughter emerged from the chaos I found,
Perhaps life's just a joke, so let's gather 'round!

So here's to the clicks and the silliness shared,
To questions and answers, some bold and some snared.
In pixels and pixels, let's all take a chance,
Embrace the absurdity, join in the dance!

Navigating the Infinite Scroll

Life is a feed, with updates galore,
Scrolling through memes, who could ask for more?
'Get rich quick schemes' and 'how to be wise,'
Click, click, refresh, what a wonderful prize!

I pondered existence with each little swipe,
Is happiness just a like? If I could type?
The wisdom of crowds, a vast ocean wide,
But mostly they argue, they bicker and bide.

Through hashtags and trends, I sought the key,
Finding my path, or just losing my spree?
Life lessons buried in gifs and in memes,
Who knew the algorithm held out for dreams?

So I scroll on forever, with joy, not despair,
Searching for laughter, for moments to share.
Embracing the chaos, the fun and the scroll,
In this endless realm, I'm finding my role!

Algorithms of Affection

My heart's like a browser, all tabs open wide,
Searching for someone, a friend or a guide.
'Find love in a click!' Oh, how they entice,
But swipe left or right, it's a game of chance dice!

What if our feelings were all coded in bits?
With heart emojis and virtual fits?
The algorithm whispers, 'This match is just right,'
But logic says love can't be just black and white!

Connection defined by a series of likes,
A meme shared in jest, can spark fonder hikes.
In pixels of passion, we dance with delight,
Who knew romance thrived in the digital light?

So let's bicker and banter with emojis galore,
Living life simply, who could ask for more?
In this crazy old world of search terms and hearts,
Love's an adventure, let the coding start!

Cybernetic Connections

I plugged in my heart, did it spark or just fade?
With cables and signals, a new plan is laid.
'Connect with your spirit!' the pop-ups suggest,
But my Wi-Fi was weak, left me feeling distressed.

Tangled in filters, my selfie on blast,
Do I look like a sage or just stuck in the past?
Each notification buzzes like life's own drum,
A symphony scattered, where's all the fun?

In forums and chat rooms, I search for some truth,
Answering riddles from my digital youth.
Could it be that wisdom's hidden in sales?
Or is it found out on some vast digital trails?

So here's to connections, both wired and free,
With laughter and glitches, let's just let it be!
In this cybernetic dance, we find our confetti,
Embracing the chaos, let's keep it all steady!

Facebook Philosophies

Scroll and stop, a life advice,
'Like' if you think it's something nice.
Memes replace the age-old sages,
Wisdom lost in digital pages.

Post a pic, and you're profound,
But jokes alone should wear the crown.
Hashtags rule, and laughter leads,
A friend request fulfills our needs.

Instructions from Infinity

Click here for wisdom, don't delay,
Infinite scroll, what do they say?
Life's a quest, download the guide,
But glitchy servers, can't abide!

Install happiness, feel the rush,
Updates roll in, don't just hush.
Pop-up ads for love and mirth,
Will we find truth on this earth?

Many-Sided Perspectives

Google says life's like a cube,
Check all sides, don't be a nube.
Rotate views, try out each face,
Searching for joy in cyberspace.

Forums discuss the height of bliss,
Quoting cats in a digital hiss.
Never forget to hit refresh,
Wisdom comes with a soft mesh.

The Browser History of Humanity

Tap 'Search' for a life review,
What if the past got a redo?
Cookies stored of what we sought,
Bookmarking moments that we forgot.

Cached tweets that shaped our fate,
Tell a story, isn't it great?
The history of a million clicks,
Life's a riddle, with funny tricks.

What's Beyond the Screen?

Click on a link, what could it mean?
A cat meme pops up, it's quite the scene.
Scroll through the feeds, search for the truth,
Life's answers await in a GIF from your youth.

In pixelated worlds, we wander and play,
Finding deep wisdom in what memes convey.
A search for the soul in a funny cat chat,
Is this the wise life? Or just a bit flat?

Wisdom in hashtags, enlightenment in tweets,
Navigating life through viral retreats.
With each little scroll, we laugh and we sigh,
Unraveling questions while we just scroll by.

So log in, dear friend, to this quest we adore,
For wisdom online is but just a click more.
Should we trust the device for answers that stick?
Or laugh at the chaos, our humorous trick?

Virtual Labyrinths of Meaning

Click here for answers, just a few clicks away,
The meaning of life? Oh, what do you say?
Page after page, we chase after bliss,
In the vast information, what did we miss?

The search bar is beckoning, a tempting delight,
Is deep understanding hiding out of sight?
With articles popping up, jam-packed with lore,
Are we lost in this maze, or is there something more?

What if the truth lives in a viral trend?
Or maybe the wisdom is just a good friend?
We find in our laughter a semblance of cause,
Could the secret be hidden in numerous paws?

Back and forth we wander, in this digital space,
Trying to capture that ever-elusive grace.
Where do we turn when our wisdom feels thin?
To the next trending topic, let the search begin!

Contextualizing Consciousness

Searching for depth in endless terrains,
Finding our purpose in whimsical gains.
Virtual discoveries, profound yet absurd,
With just a few clicks, we seek the unheard.

Life's questions arise in a meme-filled stream,
Understanding ourselves through the lens of a dream.
With hashtags and likes we dance on the brink,
What if the meaning is more than we think?

A troll in the comments, a sage from afar,
Pointing to wisdom, so near yet so far.
Is the truth just a trending topic away?
Or wrapped in a riddle that socialites say?

So here we are, pondering the strange,
Inside the confines of digital range.
Let's laugh at this puzzle, both wacky and wild,
In the search for the meaning, let's stay like a child!

Trails of Thought in Cyberspace

Navigating the web, our thoughts take a spin,
In a whirlwind of clicks, where do we begin?
Each search a rabbit hole, twisting and turning,
In fields of information, our brains are burning.

Oh, the wisdom we seek has turned into a game,
Life coaching by influencers, all sounding the same.
Is truth floating by in the comments we make?
Or lost in the memes, for sanity's sake?

A viral sensation, profoundness disguised,
As we scroll through the chaos, our minds get surprised.
With bits of enlightenment swimming like fish,
Could our quest for meaning be just a fun wish?

So ride the wave, let's giggle and gawk,
At the quirky pursuits of cyberspace talk.
In the pixel-lit dark, let's not lose our glee,
For the search itself might just set us free!